FAMILIES AROUND THE WORLD

A FAMILY IN
WEST AFRICA

Peter Otto Jacobsen
Preben Sejer Kristensen

Wayland

Families Around the World

A Family in Australia
A Family in France
A Family in Holland
A Family in Hong Kong
A Family in India
A Family in Ireland
A Family in Japan
A Family in Mexico
A Family in the Persian Gulf
A Family in Switzerland
A Family in West Africa

First published in 1985 by
Wayland (Publishers) Limited
49 Lansdowne Place, Hove
East Sussex BN3 1HF, England
© Copyright 1985 Text and photographs
Peter Otto Jacobsen and
Preben Sejer Kristensen
© Copyright 1985 English-language edition
Wayland (Publishers) Limited

ISBN 0 85078 434 4

Phototypeset by Kalligraphics Limited
Redhill, Surrey
Printed in Italy by G. Canale and C.S.p.A., Turin

Contents

Arriving in The Gambia   6

By car through Senegal   8

An African village   10

Mamat Drammeh   12

Education and religion   14

Three wives   18

Living off the land   20

Preparing a feast   24

A village celebration   26

Facts about West Africa   30

Glossary   31

Index   32

Arriving in The Gambia

We are at Yundum airport in The Gambia, waiting with our fellow arrivals for our luggage to be unloaded from the plane standing on the tarmac. It is late afternoon and the African sun is a large red globe hanging low in the sky. Its rays are strong, even at this time of day, and the air is hot and humid.

The Gambia is a tiny, narrow country stretching 480 kilometres (300 miles) inland from the Atlantic coast of West Africa. West Africa itself is divided into many territories, covering a huge area from the Sahara Desert in the west across to Chad further east, and south to the Congo and Gabon, which lie on the equator. Europeans began to explore and exploit West Africa from about the sixteenth century and some of the names of the coastal areas, such as the Ivory Coast, Gold Coast and Slave Coast, reflect the early trading.

Our luggage has been unloaded and we find our bags, then make our way to the bus waiting to take us the 27 kilometres (seventeen miles) into Banjul,

People of Banjul, the capital city of The Gambia.

Gambia's capital. Tomorrow we will continue our journey across the border into Senegal, travelling to the village of Chief Mamat Drammeh and his family.

The bus speeds along reddish, sandy roads with little traffic. On either side stretches the dry savannah landscape of rough grass and clumps of low trees dotted here and there. When the rainy season comes the savannah will be green and lush. We pass by a village of round mud huts, where a group of children have gathered at the roadside to wave and smile at us.

By the time we reach Banjul it is dark, and the sky above us is full of shining stars.

West Africa stretches about 2,500 miles (4,000 kilometres) inland, and southward for about 1,000 miles (1,600 kilometres).

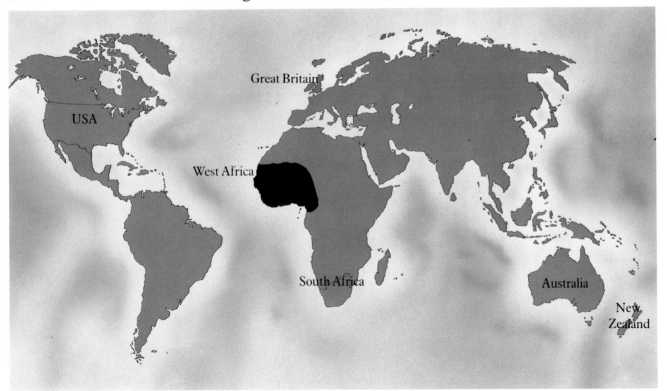

By car through Senegal

We are up very early next morning. We drive in hot sunshine through the town, which is already filling up with traffic and crowds of smiling people on their way to the market place. Many are carrying baskets on their heads with the fruit, vegetables, fish and cloth they hope to sell that day. Banjul is at the mouth of the River Gambia, on its south bank and we must take a ferry across to Barra on the north bank, before driving on across the border into Senegal.

Until 1960, when it became an independent Republic, Senegal was French territory and it still has very close ties

Shoppers and traders buy and sell a variety of goods in Banjul's market place.

with France. It is a big country, covering an area of about 200,000 square kilometres (77,000 square miles), bordered to the west by the Atlantic Ocean, to the north by Mauritania, to the east by Mali, and to the south by Guinea and Guinea-Bissau. The Gambia region is completely engulfed by Senegal.

The river crossing does not take long

and once across we lose no time and head north towards the border. In Senegal, the main roads are tarmac and to begin with we make fast progress through the flat, dry landscape. However, as we travel further into the interior the roads give way to bumpy, earth-beaten tracks, and the grassland to scrub and bush. As we jolt along the dry road, our car startles a herd of grazing gazelle and they take flight, their delicate hooves kicking up clouds of dust. As in the rest of Africa, Senegal's wildlife is mostly protected in national reserves. We have been driving for several hours now. We stop the car to look at the map, and to refresh ourselves from our water-bottles.

A family of monkeys lazily crosses the road and, ignoring us, disappears into the bush. Only the male remains, standing by the road looking angrily at us for a minute or so. It is near midday and the brilliant sun is high overhead. Vultures, who normally keep to the tree-tops, are huddled against tree stumps trying to find some shade.

Passengers boarding the ferry that crosses the River Gambia.

An African village

An hour or so later, we catch sight of a primitive water-tank up ahead and we pull over to the roadside. Hanging on the branches of a nearby tree are some old tin cans to drink from.

Opposite this little refreshment stand lies Drammeh Gahjan, the village we have come to visit. It is set back from the road and surrounded by a high straw fence. We follow the sandy path leading through an opening in the fence.

Inside, about forty mud and straw huts are arranged in small groups, with stretches of dusty earth between each group. In the middle is a kind of square, and a well for the village water supply. Here and there, a tree casts a thin shadow to give shelter from the burning sun. Cows, sheep, goats and skinny chickens are wandering to and fro.

Outside some of the huts, barefoot women and children sit cracking peanuts by smashing them on stones. Others are

Two women pounding millet.

pounding millet with large wooden clubs. When they see us they stop and watch curiously. Then an elderly man comes towards us and welcomes us to the village. His dignified bearing and noble face tell us that he must be Mamat Drammeh, chief of the village. He speaks to us in Wolof, one of the seventeen known tribal languages of Senegal. He invites us to take refreshment with him and he leads us to his hut in the centre of the village.

With the arrival of the Europeans, West Africa was divided into many different territories.

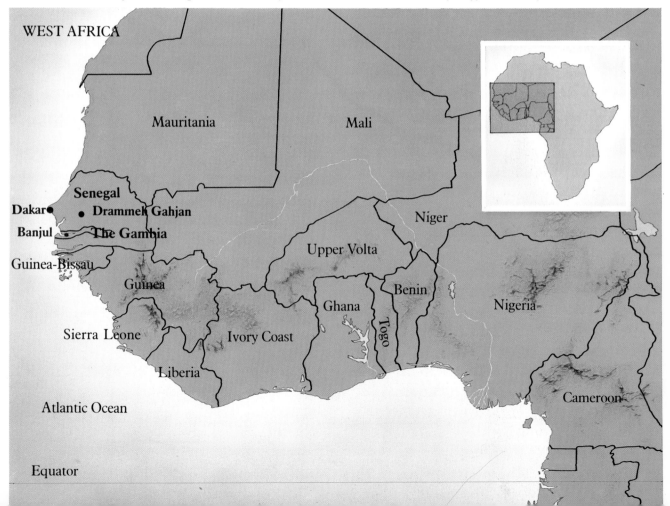

Mamat Drammeh

Like the other huts its walls are made of dried mud, and the cone-shaped roof is made from millet straw thatch, which keeps it dry when it rains and cool when it is hot. The chief's hut has a door made from hammered-out oil drums, unlike the rest of the huts in the village which have simple openings.

Inside, the chief's hut is bare of furniture apart from a bed propped up on large stones, and a low wooden bench. There are a few pots and other possessions scattered around too. Mamat hands us small cups of refreshing herbal tea, and invites us to sit on the bench. He sits on the bed, and his straight back and the red fez on his head add to his air of natural dignity and authority. We begin to ask him questions and he answers, hesitantly to begin with, in a low, gentle voice.

'My grandfather founded the village and was its first chief,' he tells us. 'I have three wives and twelve children, and my tribe is the Wolof. Many years ago we were a powerful tribe but now we are mostly peaceful farmers.'

When the Europeans arrived in West Africa they imposed a vast number of changes, including the division of the country into territories. In many cases, a tribe was split between two or three different territories.

We say we would be honoured to meet Mamat's wives.

'My youngest wife, Safou, is the only one at home. The other two have gone to market together in a nearby village,' he tells us.

Some children have gathered in the doorway and he sends one of them to fetch Safou. After a few minutes she comes into the hut, carrying one-year-old Momodou in her arms, the chief's youngest child. Like the other village women, Safou is barefoot and dressed in a long colourful robe called a *boubou*, with a piece of material wound around her head in a kind of turban - her *mousor*.

'I have seven boys and five girls,' Mamat tells us with pride. 'My oldest son is 30 years old.'

Mamat in his hut with Safou and three of his twelve children.

12

13

Education and religion

Islam is a way of life and the village children are instructed in their religion three times a day.

14

While we have been talking, the children have been listening and watching. We ask Mamat whether they go to school.

'All the village children receive some education. We have a teacher in the village who instructs them in Islam, our religion, three times a day,' he tells us.

The followers of Islam are known as Moslems. The Wolof tribe have been Moslems for several hundred years, although Islam did not become widespread in Senegal until the nineteenth century and is still an expanding religion. Today, 80% of the population are Moslems and follow one of five 'brotherhoods'. The Tidjanes and Mourids are the main ones.

'Islam's most important festival is Ramadan,' says Mamat. 'This is a month of fasting when no-one must eat or drink from daybreak until sunset. When Ramadan is over everyone celebrates with a great feast, called *Kouté*.'

There are schools, colleges and universities in the main towns and cities, but education for the bush children is a problem the authorities are trying to tackle.

Right *A mosque in Dakar, Senegal's capital city.*

15

One difficulty is that they must first learn French, since all schooling is in French. In many areas, Family Centres have been set up where children and young people are given a basic education in farming, accounts, domestic economy, childcare and diet.

'When the children are not at lessons, they help the adults in the fields or to prepare food. But they have time for play, too,' says Mamat.

We are outside in the dusty heat once more. Two small boys proudly show us toy wooden cars they have made themselves.

'We are poor people and any toys the children have are nearly always homemade,' explains Mamat.

'Tradition is strong in our village and it also has its role when it comes to the children. At fifteen years of age I send my own children away from the village to learn a craft other than farming, which of course they must also know. In this way they learn independence and on their return to the village can contribute new skills. That is how it has always been.'

Two village boys with home-made toy cars.

The authorities are trying to improve education for the bush children like those in Mamat's village.

Three wives

We ask Mamat how he met his wives.

'You have met Safou already. A messenger has gone to the next village to tell the other two of your arrival. They will be back shortly, bringing a hen. We shall have a feast today!' he says. We feel honoured at such treatment.

'I met my first wife, Haddy, when I was working as a farmer in a village in Gambia. She worked in the same place and before long we discovered we were interested in one another. That was in 1944 when I was 24 years old, and she was 12. I had to pay her family 2,000 French African francs (about £3),' Mamat told us.

Polygamy (marrying more than one wife) is permitted in Senegal, but it is not such common practice as it once was. In 1974 a new family law on marriage was passed. Polygamy is not forbidden, but a bridegroom must now make a formal choice between one or two (the maximum allowed) wives. He must sign a document stating his intention. The authorities hope this law will help limit Senegal's growing population, since families of ten or more children are all too common.

'I married my second wife, Fatou, in 1956. She was 14. The last time I married was in 1962,' Mamat says in his gentle voice.

'They think of each other as sisters and

Mamat's three wives, Haddy, Fatou and Safou.

This woman is a village chief. Today in Senegal, women are considered equal to men.

never argue,' he continues. 'They are really fond of each other. In any case, they are used to the tradition – for one man to have three wives is not strange to them.'

However, throughout Senegal, the status of women is changing and today they are considered equal to men. There are many women in the professions and four women in the country's National Assembly.

19

Living off the land

'Each family in the village must look after itself and grow enough to live on throughout the year. No-one has to pay to live in the village or work the land,' says Mamat. 'However, as chief, I give permission for a newcomer to stay. After the newcomer has built his own hut he is given land of his own.'

As village chief, Mamat decides who may settle in Drammeh Gahjan.

Mamat is a farmer, growing peanuts, cotton and millet.

21

We follow Mamat a little way out of the village to the fields where he grows peanuts, cotton and millet.

'I get up every morning at 7 o'clock. Then I wash, pray, eat breakfast and work in the fields until 7 o'clock in the evening, with only a short rest for lunch. I have done that all my life,' he says.

Farming methods are very simple and many tools have remained unchanged for centuries. Mamat uses the traditional agricultural tool of a broad-bladed, short-handled hoe.

Senegal is a not a rich country and it is basically agricultural. Its chief crop is the groundnut (or peanut), and in a good year it is a leading world producer. A lot of land is devoted to groundnuts and Senegal has to import much of the food it could be growing for itself. The authorities are trying to change this situation.

'Other crops are being more widely grown now,' says Mamat. 'Rice, sugar and, in particular, cotton are also successful. Droughts are frequent, though, and they badly affect cattle farming, for example. The government is investigating new ways of saving water by building more reservoirs and dams.

'The cotton is sold to a local textile mill,' says Mamat. 'Each year a representative from a co-operative in Dakar, the capital, comes to buy the groundnuts and millet we don't need ourselves.'

Life must be very hard for the village when there is a drought and the crops fail and we ask Mamat if the village receives outside help.

'Yes, some help,' he replies, 'and I myself receive a token sum from the authorities each year because I own the village.'

The West African territories have all gained their independence during the last thirty years. However, life is very difficult for most people and today governments and Western aid are active in trying to improve conditions by establishing better agricultural methods, health-care, education and so on.

Cattle farming in Senegal is affected disastrously whenever drought hits the land.

23

Preparing a feast

Mamat with two of his sons and one of his wives, who have returned from market.

We walk slowly back towards the village. By now everyone has heard of our presence and there is quite a gathering around the chief's hut.

Two of Mamat's wives, Haddy and Fatou, have returned from market and walk towards us accompanied by Mamat's oldest son. He is carrying a squawking hen by the legs. They smile at us in greeting and exchange a few words with Mamat.

The chief's oldest son lays the hen on the ground and cuts its throat with a knife so that it bleeds slowly. Meanwhile, Haddy, Fatou and Safou are sweeping out the kitchen hut ready to prepare the food. The hut is empty of furniture apart from pots and pans, firewood and two iron-stands for cooking. When the hen is ready, the chief's son hands it over to the women to pluck and clean.

Inside the kitchen hut, Haddy lights a fire under one of the three-legged iron stands and puts a pan of water to boil. Outside, the women cut the hen up into eight pieces which they put into water to clean. They chop onions, tomatoes, peppers, and some large snails!

'This is a celebration meal,' says Mamat. 'It is not every day that we kill a hen. Usually we eat very simply. Mostly rice or millet, and vegetables.'

The chief eats one main meal a day, in the evening. 'After I have eaten I usually relax before going to bed so that I am fresh for work the next day,' he tells us.

The ingredients are put into a pot of boiling water.

A village celebration

The whole village joins in when there is a family celebration and we notice that several of the women have changed their clothes. Many of the younger ones of marriagable age are looking at us with interest. Perhaps they think they can persuade us to settle in their village!

They grin and smile at us, and there is a real festival atmosphere. One of the women begins to bang a tomtom drum

Singing and dancing are an important part of African culture.

A festive meal – Senegalese hen served with millet.

and sing, and we watch as others join in, clapping their hands and dancing.

'When we celebrate, we eat well and sing and dance,' says Mamat.

The delicious smell of the cooking hen wafts out to us from the kitchen hut. We are very hungry. We have not eaten since early morning. By now, the sun is getting low in the sky and it is almost evening. Haddy and Fatou bring our food, which is served with a bowl of millet, cooked and presented like rice.

It tastes very good, and we sit and eat, watching the singing, dancing people. The scene is almost perfect but we know that these people are poor and their lives are hard. We ask Mamat if he has any hopes or plans for the future. He is silent for a moment and then he shakes his head.

'I am 61 years old – an old man. When I was young, I would get angry about the unfair things in life. Now, though, I am happy. I worked hard when I was young and I had good and bad experiences like every man. Today I am content, I have no more ambitions left.'

A gentle smile lights up the chief's face. He is a deep-thinking man and we do not doubt the wisdom of his words.

By now it is dusk and we must leave. Mamat invites us to stay but we reluctantly say no, explaining that we have to be at the airport the next day. We say goodbye to Mamat and thank him for his kindness and hospitality. Haddy, Fatou, Safou and the children are waiting to say goodbye too, with many of the villagers. We feel sad to be leaving this beautiful and peaceful village and its friendly, hospitable people.

Mamat and his villagers walk with us to the car. We say more goodbyes and they wave and smile as we drive off into the African wilderness.

The wise chief, Mamat Drammeh, and some of his children.

Facts about West Africa

Senegal
Size: 200,000 sq. km. (77,000 sq. mi.). **Capital city** : Dakar. **Population:** 5.5 million.

The Gambia
Size: 10,360 sq. km. (4,000 sq. mi.). **Capital city:** Banjul. **Population:** 620,000.

Mauritania
Size: 1,085,805 sq. km. (419,232 sq. mi.). **Capital city:** Nouakchott. **Population:** 1.5 million.

Mali
Size: 1,204,350 sq. km. (465,000 sq. mi.). **Capital city:** Bamako. **Population:** 6.5 million.

Guinea
Size: 250,880 sq. km. (96,865 sq. mi.). **Capital city:** Conakry. **Population:** 5.25 million.

Sierra Leone
Size: 73,325 sq. km. (27,925 sq. mi.). **Capital city:** Freetown. **Population:** 3 million.

Liberia
Size: 111,370 sq. km. (43,000 sq. mi.). **Capital city:** Monrovia. **Population:** 1.75 million.

Ivory Coast
Size: 328,900 sq. km. (127,000 sq. mi.). **Capital city:** Abidjan. **Population:** 8.1 million.

Upper Volta
Size: 274,500 sq. km. (105,900 sq. mi.). **Capital city:** Ouagadougou. **Population:** 6.4 million.

Ghana
Size: 237,873 sq. km. (91,843 sq. mi.). **Capital city:** Accra. **Population:** 8.5 million.

Togo
Size: 54,390 sq. km. (21,000 sq. mi.). **Capital city:** Lome. **Population:** 2.6 million.

Benin
Size: 111,970 sq. km. (43,232 sq. mi.). **Capital city:** Porto Novo. **Population:** 3.6 million.

Nigeria
Size: 923,768 sq. km. (356,669 sq. mi.). **Capital city:** Lagos. **Population:** 90 million.

Niger
Size: 1,191,400 sq. km. (460,000 sq. mi.). **Capital city:** Niamey. **Population:** 4 million.

Glossary

Cameroon
Size: 475,400 sq. km. (183,000 sq. mi.). **Capital city:** Yaounde. **Population:** 8.5 million.

Language: In eight countries, French is the official language, in five countries English is the official language, in Mauritania the official language is Arabic. Other languages are tribal.

Religion: Islam is the strongest religion throughout West Africa. Christianity and tribal religions are also followed.

Climate: The climate ranges from tropical to equatorial.

Agriculture: Groundnuts, rice, millet, coffee, cocoa, palm products, fishing, timber.

Industry: Iron-ore mining, fishing, food-processing, diamonds, gold, rubber, bauxite, phosphates, oil, uranium.

Drought A serious lack of rain or water.
Interior *or* bush Wild, rough country.
Islam The religion of Moslems, which teaches that there is only one God and that his prophet is Mohammed.
Koran The sacred scriptures of Islam.
Millet A grain plant, grown for food.
Polygamy The custom of having more than one wife or husband at the same time.
Savannah Open grasslands with scattered bushes or trees.

Acknowledgements

All the illustrations in this book were supplied by the authors with the exception of the following: Camerapix/Alan Hutchison 6, 8, 9, 10, 15, 19, 23. The maps on pages 7 and 11 were drawn by Bill Donohoe.

Index

Banjul 6, 7–8
Barra 8

Celebration 15, 26–8
Cooking 25–7
Cooking ingredients 25
Cooking utensils 25
Cotton 22
Crops 22

Dakar 22
Drammeh Gahjan 10
Drought 22

Education 15–16, 22

Family centres 16
Farming 16, 22
Fatou 18, 25, 27
Feast 18, 24–5
Food 25, 28
France 8
French language 16

Gambia, The 6
Groundnuts (peanuts) 10, 22

Haddy 18, 25, 27
Health-care 22
Huts 7, 10, 12, 20

Islam 15

Kitchen hut 25, 28

Mamet Drammeh, Chief 7, 11–
   12, 15–16, 20, 25
Millet 11
Momodou 12
Monkeys 9
Moslems 15

National Assembly 19

Polygamy 18
Population 18

Ramadan 15

Safou 12, 18, 25
Sahara Desert 6
Savannah 7
Senegal 7, 9, 11, 15, 22

Tomtom 27
Tribal boundaries 12
Tribes 12

Village 7, 10–11, 20
Villagers 20, 28
Vultures 9

Well 10
West African Territories 22
Western aid 22
Wildlife 9
Wives 12, 18–19
Wolof language 11
Wolof Tribe 12, 15
Women, status of 19